The Shroud of Turin Speaks for Itself

*Simon Brown
and Co-author Caspar McCloud*

1st Edition
© 5/2013
Revised 9/23/2013

Simon Brown
www.realdiscoveries.info

Edited and Published by:
Life Application Ministries Publishing
(LAMP)

Also edited by: Gaynor Barradell and
Caspar McCloud

www.LAMPublishing.org

Cover Design: LAMP
Cover Shroud Photo: ©1978 Barrie M.
Schwortz Collection, STERA, Inc.

Printer: createspace.com

All scripture was taken from the King
James Version - 2000 Bible (©2003)

Special Acknowledgements

I want to first of all, thank my Lord Jesus Christ for saving me and helping me with these discoveries so I can share the great finds with others.

To my wife who has been with me to all hours of the night as I researched, traveled, and spent time writing my findings.

To my co-author and friend, Caspar McCloud, who edited, provided insights and teachings that inspired me to create the book in the first place.

To Linda Lange (Life Application Ministries Publishing), who showed great dedication in putting this book together. Without her expertise this book wouldn't have become a reality.

And to Gaynor Barradell. Her quick turn around in the initial editing helped get the book off the ground.

And thanks to Roly and Rosie of http://www.millennium3music.co.uk who also helped with the initial editing.

May you be blessed with
this book for the Glory of God
through Jesus Christ,
Amen.

Index

Preface 7

Chapter One - Evidence of Authenticity ... 11

Chapter Two - The Garden Tomb and the Shroud are Linked 20

Chapter Three - Passover Resurrection Message 32

Chapter Four - Faith in God 36

Chapter Five - Finding the Tomb of Jesus 46

Chapter Six - Linen Cloths 57

Chapter Seven - What is the Point of the Shroud? 66

Chapter Eight - Pastor Caspar's Message of the Resurrection of Jesus 76

Prayer for Salvation 81

My Prayer for You 83

About the Author - Simon Brown 85

About the Co-Author - Caspar McCloud 88

About the Free DVD offer 91

Other Books and Resources 93

Contact Information 95

Footnote References 96

Preface

Every good gift and every perfect gift is from above, and cometh down from the Father of lights, with whom is no variableness, neither shadow of turning.
(James 1:17)

As stated above by our brother James (the half brother of Jesus Christ) this scripture conveys the profound truth that God the Father has truly given us the greatest gift from above, His only begotten Son; Who not only lived a perfect and sinless life, but also paid for all of our sins. He has made it possible for all those who believe in Him and turn away from their sins, follow Him and be covered by His mercy, grace, and love so that they may inherit eternal life with Christ.

Just as I consider *The Shroud of Turin* to be a gift from God above, I believe it establishes scientific and historical proof of the reliability of the Bible and also perhaps—just for the skeptics and doubting Thomas's—the supernatural evidence of God's love for humans. This Shroud gives us physical evidence of the

The Shroud of Turin Speaks for Itself

death of His only begotten Son, Jesus—by crucifixion—the recorded graphic detail of a supernatural picture of the pain and suffering He endured on the cross.

The image on the shroud reveals the torture of the forty lashes, shows us the scars and pierced body, and the painful puncture wounds from the crown of thorns which pierced His head. It shows us His plucked out beard and records His humiliation by the Romans, who punched and bruised His swollen cheekbones. It shows His pain from carrying His own cross, which can be seen by the damaged knee from falling. It shows His agony from the blood shed of His pierced hands and feet that bears silent witness to the horror of the cross. It bears the spear wound in His side, and yes, the ultimate triumph of the Resurrection of Jesus (Yeshua) meaning *Salvation*. All this is recorded supernaturally on *The Shroud of Turin.*

Special Thanks To El Centro Español de Sindonología es una Asociación for this Image

Could we give up our own child to extreme suffering for somebody else's evil deeds? The evil deeds of people who are guilty, deeds that some of us would condemn a person for forever? Could we even sacrifice our only child to die for others who are good, or yet, bad?

> John 3:16 *For God so loved the world that He gave His only begotten Son, that whosoever believes in Him, should not perish but have everlasting life.*

Here in John 3:16, told by Jesus—the Creator and the Maker of the Universe—that the highest act, the highest expression, and the highest manner is the depth of love of God the Father towards all humankind since the beginning of the world. This is His unmerited gift to mankind, a gift that no man has earned or deserved.

> Ephesians 2:8 *For by grace are ye saved through faith; and that not of yourselves: it is the gift of God*:

This is true love—there cannot be any higher love expressed by the Most High Creator of the world. We were lost in darkness, but the Lord God of Abraham, Isaac, and Jacob demonstrates to the human race the greatest deed which no man can truly comprehend—all visible on *The Shroud of Turin*.

Just as Paul writes in 1 Thessalonians 5:21 says, *"Test all things; hold fast that which is good."*

The Shroud of Turin is the most tested and analyzed single artifact in the world. It has passed and proved to be good. It has passed and proved to be the actual cloth used by Joseph of Arimathea to cover the body of Jesus Christ.

The research provided in this book is extensive because we wanted to provide the best possible information to help you see the truth. Our goal is to point you to the only begotten Son Who is able to save your soul. So, let us go straight to the facts and findings about...

The Shroud of Turin

Shroud of Turin and Barrie M. Schwortz ©1978 Barrie M. Schwortz Collection, STERA, Inc., All Rights Reserved

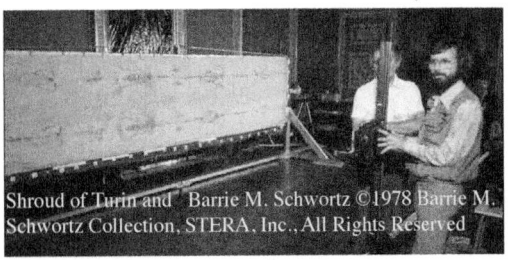

Chapter One

Evidence of Authenticity

After the radiocarbon dating test in 1988, the results of the Shroud proved it to be a medieval date of 1260-1390. Subsequently, scientists have now proved that the corner from which the radiocarbon sample had been taken was in fact a re-woven, patched, or repaired corner which was newer than the original cloth.

Marino Benford's and Sue Benford's[1] brilliant bit of detective work discovered clear indications of a discrete repair to the Shroud.

Ray Rogers[2] was an explosive research expert and thermal analyst with the Los Alamos Scientific Laboratory for over thirty years before serving on the Department of the Air Force Scientific Advisory Board, where he held the equivalent rank of Lt. General and earned a Distinguished Service Award. Ray Rogers wasn't just a scientist—he was one of America's finest. He was also part of the original *Shroud of Turin* research team in 1978.

The Shroud of Turin Speaks for Itself

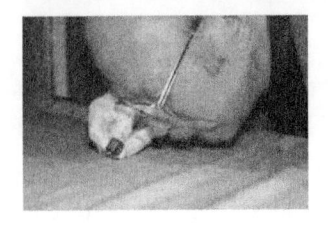

RAY ROGERS © 2002 Raymond Rogers Collection, STERA, Inc.. All Rights Reserved

Ray Rogers, who was an Atheist that originally believed the Shroud was a hoax, converted to believing it was genuine after discovering Madder root dye and gum on the fibers of the Shroud. This is clear evidence of the careful mending of the Shroud that was intended to be imperceptible and of a thread indicating a medieval repair.

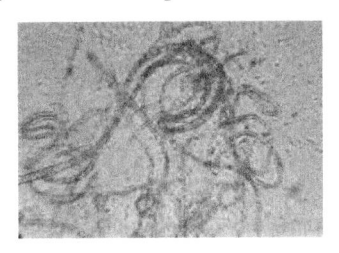

Madder root dye and gum on fibres. This is clear evidence of careful mending intended to be imperceptible. © 2002 Raymond Rogers Collection, STERA, Inc. All Rights Reserved

Evidence of Authenticity

Pete Shumacher[3], the inventor of the NASA VP-8 Image Analyzer, discovered a 3D topographical image which showed very clearly the image of a man in three dimensions proving it was not a painting but that the cloth had been wrapped around a real person.

The topographical 3 d image of the Shroud created by the VP-8 computer ©1978 Barrie M. Schwortz Collection, STERA, Inc., All Rights Reserved.

Barrie Schworz[4] stated that the wealth of evidence gathered by his team indicated that the Shroud was not a fake, that it was not a medieval painting, forgery, hoax, photograph, rubbing, etching, or dust painting.

The results of this research has been published in peer-reviewed scientific journals, including those of Archeological Chemistry: Organic, Inorganic, and Biochemical Analysis,

American Chemical Society, Applied Optics and the Canadian Society of Forensic Sciences Journal.

After testing the bloodstains on the Shroud, the tests revealed that they were indeed human bloodstains. The shroud shows the bloodstains of the crucifixion near the wrists of the man to be forensically accurate—unlike all medieval and renaissance art, which shows the crucifixion holes in the hands which is not correct.

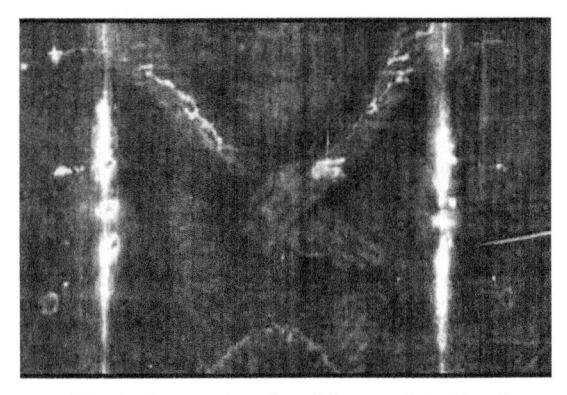

Blood stains near the wrists of the man of the Shroud.
©1978 Barrie M. Schwortz Collection, STERA, Inc.,
All Rights Reserve

The thumbs of the crucified man on the Shroud are not visible. This would have been caused by median nerve damage as the nails passed through the spaces of Destot, causing the thumbs to turn in.

The vertical flow of the bloodstains on the Shroud proved to be in perfect forensic agreement with the blood flow of a crucified man who is positioned vertically on a cross.

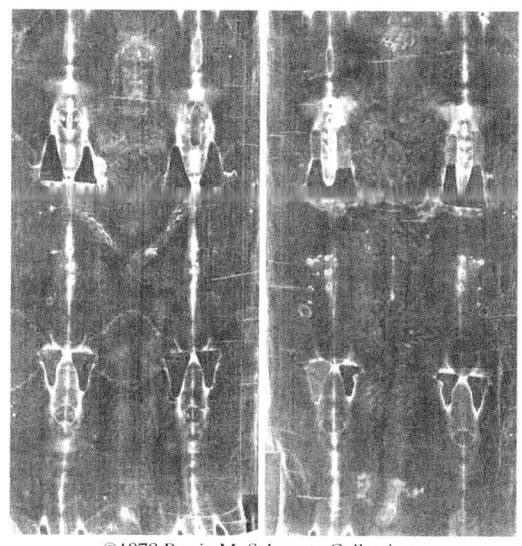

©1978 Barrie M. Schwortz Collection,
STERA, Inc., All Rights Reserve

Each blood stain on the Shroud shows the image of a lead weight at the end of each whip lash.

> Isaiah 50:6 *I gave my back to the smiters, and my cheeks to them that plucked out the beard: I hid not my face from shame and spitting.*

Does The Shroud of Turin show any facial hairs missing?

Barrie Schwartz[5], official photographer of *The Shroud of Turin* says, "YES."

The "Hungarian Prayer Manuscript" known as "The Codex Pray[6]" or "The Pray Codex," was discovered in 1770. Inside this most prominent document is an old handwritten Hungarian text dating back to 1192 that shows the following five illustrations:

1. Jesus was entirely naked with His arms on His pelvis, identical to *The Shroud of Turin*.

2. The woven fabric of a cloth showing a herringbone pattern, identical to the weaving pattern of *The Shroud of Turin*.

Evidence of Authenticity

3. Another illustration shows one piece of cloth that was identical to *The Shroud of Turin*.

4. An illustration showing "poker holes" identical to the "poker holes" on *The Shroud of Turin*.

5. The Hungarian Prayer Manuscript serves as evidence for the existence of The *Shroud of Turin* and its ability to pre-date the radiocarbon 14 dating of The Shroud of Turin in 1988.

The bloodstains on the Shroud clearly correspond to the wounds of a man who has been whipped and scourged before being crucified.

Experts who have studied the Shroud estimate around 120 scourge marks on the body, front and back, consistent with "40 lashes" from a three-thronged whip; "40 lashes" was the correct amount the Romans used.

The Shroud was not created by any artistic means currently known to mankind. All of the research team's tests indicated that the Shroud was a genuine burial cloth.

Directly near the heart is the darkest blood

stain of all, which we call the 'spear wound' blood stain that appears on the Shroud.

The 'spear wound' on the Shroud is in perfect forensic agreement with John 19:34 that says: *But one of the soldiers with a spear pierced his side, and forthwith came there out blood and water.*

The researchers discovered that if the Shroud was a fake, it must have been created by an artist with a comprehensive understanding of the forensics of crucifixion—something that virtually no other artists of that period have demonstrated.

There are bloodstains on the Shroud on the head as if from a cap—or "crown"—of thorns.

The bloodstains are the "crown" of thorns on the Shroud which is in perfect forensic agreement with John 19:2 that says: *And the soldiers platted a crown of thorns, and put it on his head.*

Everything about *The Shroud of Turin*—all the bloodstains, all the markings—these are all accurate to the gospel account of what was done to Jesus when He was scourged, beaten, crucified and then speared in the side.

Evidence of Authenticity

When we look at the face on the Shroud, we see the bruised cheek bones—one more swollen than the other—but both noticeably swollen.

The evidence of the bruised cheek bones on the Shroud is in perfect forensic agreement with John 18:22 saying: *And when he had thus spoken, one of the officers which stood by struck Jesus with the palm of his hand.*

What the Shroud gives us is a forensically accurate description of a crucified man, exactly as the gospel accounts recorded the death of Jesus, which is physical, undisputable, scientific proof of the crucifixion.

Chapter Two

The Garden Tomb and the Shroud are Linked

The Burial of Jesus

Matthew 27:57-61 *[57]As evening approached, there came a rich man from Arimathea, named Joseph, who had himself become a disciple of Jesus. [58]Going to Pilate, he asked for Jesus' body, and Pilate ordered that it be given to him. [59]Joseph took the body, wrapped it in a clean linen cloth, [60]and placed it in his own new tomb that he had cut out of the rock. He rolled a big stone in front of the entrance to the tomb and went away. [61]Mary Magdalene and the other Mary were sitting there opposite the tomb.*

Scientists say the Shroud was created by a flash of supernatural light. Italian researchers now believe the burial cloth is authentic because of the evidence and the kind of technology needed to create a 3D image of Jesus on a single piece of cloth.

The Montreal Gazette[7] announces that scientists say that The Shroud of Turin could not have been faked.

In 2007, I created a documentary called *"Our search for the Tomb of Jesus.[8]"* In this documentary I contacted 10 Shroud scholars who all stated that the person in *The Shroud of Turin* was about 5 ft. 11 inches tall.

Imposed picture placing the Shroud in the Tomb, measuring the exact size of the Tomb[9].

The Shroud of Turin Speaks for Itself

Peter from Simon's team measuring the grave of Jesus in the Garden Tomb, which conforms exactly to the height of the man on the Shroud which is about 5 ft. 11 inches tall[9].

A closeup of the sepulchre of Jesus showing the grave area to be cut out for Jesus' body as Jesus was taller than Joseph of Arimathea[9].

Barrie Schwartz states, "The question about the Garden Tomb is an interesting one. The first thing I have to admit is that I have not done a true study of the Garden Tomb myself, but understanding that the height of the tomb is 5 ft. 11 inches is certainly coincidental with what I have always perceived that the average height of the man on the shroud is—5 ft. 11 inches."

Mechthild Flury Lemberg[10]—a Textile expert—discovered clear evidence at Mount Masada of a surprisingly similar cloth that was found—made at the same time as the Shroud and dating back to the time of Jesus.

Mechthild Flury Lemberg also stressed how the Shroud had been preserved so well. She stated it was unexplainable; similar cloths she has seen—dating around the same time—are almost unrecognizable.

Jesus was Wrapped in Two Cloths

Did God preserve the Shroud Himself for such a time as this?

> 2 Peter 3:3 *Knowing this first, that there shall come in the last days scoffers, walking after their own lusts.*

The gospels clearly identify the burial cloth of Jesus' body to be one single cloth.

> Luke 23:53 *And having taken it down, he wrapped it in a clean linen cloth.*

Please note "A clean linen cloth."

> Matthew 27:59 *And when Joseph had taken the body, he wrapped it in a clean linen cloth,*

The gospels clearly identify the face cloth of Jesus and the napkin that was around his head—Sudarium of Oviedo (napkin) that was about His head was wrapped in a place by itself.

> John 20:7 *And the napkin, that was about his head, not lying with the*

linen clothes, but wrapped together in a place by itself.

There were two cloths found in the tomb where Jesus was laid. One is called The *Sudarium of Oviedo* which is a face cloth. The other is *The Shroud of Turin* which is the larger cloth. Both were used as Jesus' burial clothes.

My goal is to help people understand the value of both of these cloths. And I will start by telling you that both *The Shroud of Turin* and the *Sudarium of Oviedo* have been tested to have the same blood type, indicating they covered the same body.

It's important that you have a clear picture of these two cloths. I will share with you as it is described on the Wikipedia on-line dictionary[11]:

> The *Sudarium of Oviedo*, or *Shroud of Oviedo*, is a bloodstained cloth, measuring c. 84 x 53 cm, kept in the Cámara Santa of the Cathedral of San Salvador, Oviedo, Spain.[1] The Sudarium (Latin for sweat cloth) is claimed to be the cloth wrapped around the head of Jesus Christ after He died, as mentioned in the Gospel of John

(20:6-7). The small chapel housing it was built specifically for the cloth by King Alfonso II of Asturias in AD 840; the Arca Santa is an elaborate reliquary chest with a Roman esquemetal frontal for the storage of the Sudarium and other relics. The Sudarium is displayed to the public three times a year: Good Friday, the Feast of the Triumph of the Cross on 14 September, and its octave on 21 September.

Many of the stains on the Sudarium match those on the head portion of the Shroud of Turin. The Shroud had been carbon-dated (1988) to the 14th century. It has been proven by chemical studies that the segment of the cloth used in the 1988 carbon dating is not the same chemically as the rest of the linen Shroud as published in the peer-reviewed renowned scientific journal Thermochimica Acta. The claim the sample came from the Middle Ages is disputed by in a book by Joe Nickel, an author who holds degrees in the Humanities but not in Science. Blood tests done on both the Sudarium and the Shroud confirmed that the bloodstains on both cloths were of the same type: AB, a common blood type among Middle Eastern people but fairly rare among medieval Europeans. The presence of blood on the Shroud was proven by the STURP scientists and experts who studied the linen cloth and catalogued its data. Some claim there is no evidence that the shroud has the same blood type as the Sudarium, and the blood may be from an unrelated person handling the shroud centuries later.

This a picture of the ark that contains the
Sudarium of Oviedo[12]
©1978 Mark Evans Collection, STERA, Inc.
All Rights Reserved

The Shroud of Turin: as described in the free online encyclopedia[13] that says:

> *"The Shroud of Turin* or Turin Shroud (Italian: Sindone di Torino, Sacra Sindone) is a linen cloth bearing the image of a man who appears to have suffered physical trauma in a manner consistent with crucifixion. It is kept in the royal chapel of the Cathedral of Saint John the Baptist in Turin, northern Italy. The image on the shroud is commonly associated with Jesus Christ, His crucifixion and burial. It is much clearer in black-and-white negative than in its natural sepia color. The negative image was first observed in 1898, on the reverse photographic plate of amateur photographer Secondo Pia, who was allowed to photograph it while it was being exhibited in the Turin Cathedral.
>
> The origins of the shroud and its image are the subject of intense debate among scientists, theologians, historians and researchers. Scientific and popular publications have presented diverse arguments for both authenticity and possible methods of forgery. A variety of scientific theories regarding the

shroud have since been proposed, based on disciplines ranging from chemistry to biology and medical forensics to optical image analysis. The Catholic Church has neither formally endorsed nor rejected the shroud, but in 1958 Pope Pius XII approved of the image in association with the Roman Catholic devotion to the Holy Face of Jesus.

In 1978, a detailed examination was carried out by a team of American scientists called STURP. STURP found no reliable evidence of forgery, and called the question of how the image was formed "a mystery". In 1988 a radiocarbon dating test was performed on small samples of the shroud. The laboratories at the University of Oxford, the University of Arizona, and the Swiss Federal Institute of Technology, concurred that the samples they tested dated from the Middle Ages, between 1260 and 1390. In 2008 a former STURP member stated that sample was representative of the whole shroud.

According to former Nature editor Philip Ball, "it's fair to say that, despite the seemingly definitive tests in 1988, the status of the Shroud of Turin is murkier than ever. Not least, the nature of the image and how it was fixed on the cloth remain deeply puzzling." The shroud continues to remain one of the most studied and controversial artifacts in human history."

It seems God always provides further and deeper proof, with extra evidence as a second backup, to prove the reliability of His Word.

Just as God has revealed the split rock in Horeb, as told in Exodus 17:6—proving the true location of Mount Sinai—and just as God revealed the Great Stone of Mark 16:4—proving the true tomb of Jesus—God has also revealed the *Sudarium of Oviedo* which would prove that the burial cloth of Jesus is in fact *The Shroud of Turin*.

So He has given us *The Shroud of Turin* to prove the accuracy and the reliability of His Holy Bible.

Even without the evidence of the Shroud, we know the Bible is true simply because of the lives that are forever changed for the better. Every day all around the world when people accept Jesus (Yeshua), they are blessed and find true peace. Countless lives are restored, and there are countless testimonies of supernatural healings and miracles that continue like those recorded in the book of Acts. God has not changed, and His salvation plan includes healings and miracles.

> Psalm 103:1-3 [1]*Bless the Lord, O my soul: and all that is within me, bless his holy name.* [2]*Bless the Lord, O my soul, and forget not all his benefits:* [3]*Who forgiveth all thine iniquities; who healeth all thy diseases;*

I am thoroughly convinced, and I hope you are convinced too by the time you finish reading this, that *The Shroud of Turin* IS genuine. It links the Garden Tomb with the Shroud, supporting only one Doctrine which is Christianity, in the Name of The Father, The Son, and The Holy Spirit.

Chapter Three

Passover Resurrection Day Message of *The Shroud of Turin* by Simon Brown

Jesus is alive, and here is the proof! Amen

Romans 14:16 *Let not then your good be evil spoken of:*

I have written a personal message to you on a most urgent matter. I will not hesitate to stand up for what I believe is good, true, and right, and I will attempt to write this in the firm spirit of Jesus Christ of Nazareth.

Although some believers are not as interested or do not study as the Bereans did, I am proud to support the belief that *The Shroud of Turin* is in fact genuine and is the burial cloth of Jesus, as preserved by God.

Believers believe that the Bible is true and is the Word of the living God of Abraham, Isaac and Jacob. Yahweh spoken of by His Son the Living Word (Yeshua), and revealed by and through God's chosen prophets and true disciples—which the gospels clearly talk about—is God.

This teaches us of the two cloths that Joseph of Arimathea used for the burial of Jesus which existed at that time and can only be the authentic *Shroud Of Turin* and the *Sudarium of Oviedo*, which are still in existence today.

> *Luke 23:53 And having taken it down, he wrapped it in a clean linen cloth.*

The Greek word *Sudarium of Oviedo* is translated into English as "**Napkin.**"

Sudarium of Oviedo: The **napkin** that was about His head was wrapped in a place by itself.

> John 20:7 *And the napkin, that was about his head, not lying with the linen clothes, but wrapped together in a place by itself.*

Also found in: Matthew 27:59

And when Joseph had taken the body, he wrapped it in a clean linen cloth.

So, from the scriptures we see that the Shroud is a large piece of linen cloth, and the *Sudarium of Oviedo* is a smaller cloth that was wrapped around the head of Jesus.

The Shroud of Turin and *Sudarium of Oviedo* were found in the tomb.

> John 20:6-7 *⁶Then cometh Simon Peter following him, and went into the sepulchre, and seeth the linen clothes lie...*

The Shroud should not be worshipped in any way, but it is strong evidence to be used to confirm a Christian's faith in a tangible and physical way. It can also be used to bring others, who require proof, to a knowledge of God's saving grace.

As Christians, we worship nothing but Jesus Christ of Nazareth (Yeshua), Who is the foundation of our faith.

I believe the Shroud was genuinely preserved by God, because God knew that many rebellious hearts would refuse to believe that He sent His only Son to become our Great High Priest and pay the ultimate and perfect sacrifice for us. He knew some would refuse to believe that the "Lamb of God"—Who takes away the sins of the world—would replace the Old Testament animal sacrifices.

John 1:29 *The next day John seeth Jesus coming unto him, and saith, Behold the Lamb of God, which taketh away the sin of the world.*

It is also evident that most of the world does not believe that Jesus is the Christ (Yeshua)—the promised Messiah—as stated in:

2 Corinthians 4:4 *The god of this age has blinded the minds of unbelievers, so that they cannot see the light of the gospel of the glory of Christ, who is the image of God.*

Chapter Four

Faith in God

The Bible tells us that without faith in the crucifixion and resurrection of Jesus it is impossible to be saved.

> Ephesians 2:8 *For by grace are you saved through faith; and that not of yourselves: it is the gift of God.*

The Bible says if there is no resurrection of Jesus, then the preaching is in vain.

> 1 Corinthians 15:12-14 *[12]Now if Christ be preached that he rose from the dead, how say some among you that there is no resurrection of the dead? [13]But if there be no resurrection of the dead, then is Christ not risen: [14]And if Christ be not risen, then is our preaching vain, and your faith is also vain.*

Perhaps this is why God preserved and recorded the crucifixion and resurrection of Jesus on His burial clothes—*The Shroud of Turin*—something that is capable of being perceived by the mind and evidently fresh and visible to the human eye?

During the most important event in history—the death and resurrection of Jesus Christ of Nazareth—the image was frozen in time and recorded on two linen cloths for all humans to see, perceive, and understand. And in understanding, whosoever would believe and follow that very Person on the cloth, would realize that their sins had been paid for, as we find in John 3:16:

For God so loved the world (you), that he gave his only begotten Son (Jesus), that whosoever believeth in him should not perish, but have everlasting life.

If we only believe

It is as if God supplied all the evidence we needed by confirming His Holy Word—the Holy Bible. From the Shroud, God the Father and Creator of the universe has revealed His great love and made it possible for us to know the truth. Who, if they believe, receive, and follow Jesus, are granted eternal life, so that on judgment day no one can say or ask the question, "Why were we not told?"

Matthew 24:14 *And this gospel of the kingdom shall be preached in all the world for a witness unto all nations; and then shall the end come.*

Believers Who Act Like Atheists

There are things in the world that do not appear fair and there are those who have been quite unfair regarding the extraordinary physical evidence recorded of Jesus on His burial cloths.

It is a mystery which I am learning to understand from the Scriptures, asking the question show me LORD in your Holy Word.

Why are there professing born again spirit-filled Christians and worse still certain fundamentalist type Christian ministries, who almost act like atheists at times? Why are there believers who seem to condemn the only physical evidence outside the Bible of the crucifixion of Jesus?

Yes, the physical, most vital evidence that can help lost souls find faith in Jesus.

Are these believers who debunk the Shroud actually suggesting that the devil made the image of the Shroud?

Interestingly enough, the Lord showed me 2 Timothy 2:24-26:

> [24]*And the servant of the Lord must not strive; but be gentle unto all men, apt to teach, patient,* [25]*In meekness instructing those that oppose themselves; if God peradventure will give them repentance to the acknowledging of the truth;* [26]*And that they may recover themselves out of the snare of the devil, who are taken captive by him at his will.*

Because clearly we can see from these Bible verses that the enemy of our souls has taken captive believers in certain areas of their lives. Maybe they have been deeply hurt and wounded and so they entertain a spirit of bitterness and so defile those around them now.

The enemy has programmed them through lies and deceptions coming through vain imagination of unclean spirits in their thought life and in their generations that try to pull them away from the truth of God's Holy Word. We pray the Lord be merciful to those who oppose the truth and themselves for that matter.

Hebrews 12:14-25 *[14]Follow peace with all men, and holiness, without which no man shall see the Lord: [15]Looking diligently lest any man fail of the grace of God; lest any root of bitterness springing up trouble you, and thereby many be defiled;*

The Shroud of Turin clearly reveals the physical and visible evidence of the crucifixion and resurrection of Jesus Christ, which is the foundation of the Christian faith. Once we obtain this faith, we surrender our whole life to the Lord Jesus Christ by trusting, seeking, repenting, and confessing Him as our Lord and Savior, which is required to save our souls.

However, it is most vital and serious that we follow the true Jesus Christ. This, then, needs proper and reliable research for each and every believer. Wrong research will lead to the wrong faith, which will lead to dissolution and destruction.

2 Thessalonians 2:11 *And for this cause God shall send them a strong delusion, that they should believe a lie:*

How is it possible for believers to teach that

Jesus was crucified to save humans from their sins yet also teach that the two most important and significant cloths in the history of mankind are not authentic?

They believe *The Shroud of Turin* and the *Sudarium of Oviedo*—the physical and visible evidence of the four gospels of the risen Jesus Christ and the world's most famous relics which do not contradict the Bible, but prove and confirm it, forensically, accurately, scientifically, and precisely in every detail—are nothing but fakes.

We see most of the world accepting and believing in Darwin's theory of Evolution, which is exactly what it is—A THEORY. Why? Because "The Missing Link" has never been found, and never will be. Evolution is biologically impossible. It is like saying 1+1 = 10000000000000000000000000000000000.

In other words, it's absolutely impossible.

But Darwinism, like every false teaching and religion, is necessary to help kill, steal, and destroy faith and nations—which history has now proven. It is the very foundation laid for Communism to build upon.

The Shroud of Turin Speaks for Itself

> The Lord Jesus said in John 10:10: *The thief cometh not, but for to steal, and to kill, and to destroy: I am come that they might have life, and that they might have it more abundantly.*

It is said that a staggering 95% of the population are not born again. This is no surprise. Evolution is being taught to most children in schools as fact, when it is clearly not. How God's heart must grieve. There appears a sinister agenda in Academia today so that any deep thinkers or professors who challenge the theory of evolution with the idea of intelligent design will risk losing their tenure.

I suggest you see the film, "Expelled: No Intelligence Allowed[14]." Ben Stein examines the issue of academic freedom and decides that there is none at all when it comes to the debate over Intelligent design. For those who pay close attention, Stein's debate with atheist Richard Dawkins shows that Professor Dawkins has no real answers as to how life began, and the best he can come up with, from his well-educated mind, is to side with the basic tenants of New Agers, who believe some aliens from a distant galaxy started life on this planet.

I suggest reading the Bible to find the truth about the Nephilim and extraterrestrials that are, in fact, only fallen angels and demons. Seek the truth for yourself!

Matthew 7:7 *Seek, and you shall find; knock, and it shall be opened unto you.*

God had already known that most of the world would refuse to accept His Son. Could it be the reason the disciples went out of their way to hide and preserve the two cloths containing physical evidence of Jesus for us to see today?

There is now evidence which reveals that the disciples hid the Shroud and *Sudarium of Oviedo* in caves for safekeeping. Historian C. Bernard Ruffin[15] reveals recent scientific discoveries, including evidence, that the disciples themselves may have kept the cloths hidden and that Jesus recovered the Shroud from the Tomb, handing it to a follower of St. James. We are certain the *Sudarium of Oviedo* was indeed precious and important, because it was hidden and preserved with official documents in a great wooden ark.

We see *The Shroud of Turin*, now believed by atheists and scientists (including NASA), to be impossible to have been created. This position strengthens the belief of some—for example, the Muslims—who say that God has no Son. Yet the Shroud proves the greatest miracle of all: God does have a Son, and His Name is Jesus. But, sadly, the enemy of our souls has blinded the eyes and dulled the ears of certain professing believers who do not understand and so they continue to encourage others not to believe the overwhelming evidence.

> Matthew 13:15 *For this people's heart is waxed gross, and their ears are dull of hearing, and their eyes they have closed; lest at any time they should see with their eyes, and hear with their ears, and should understand with their heart, and should be converted, and I should heal them.*

Certain believers tell me I am wrong for teaching about the Shroud. I now ask them to talk to God and have a fight with Him for preserving and revealing the evidence of His Son Jesus (Yeshua) on the Shroud.

I find it can be very challenging when those who claim to be Christians attack me for simply trying to share the Gospel and prove the existence of Christ.

The fact is, most of the world does not believe the Shroud to be genuine. This gives them another reason not to believe in the Person on the cloth, Who is the only Person Who can save them. They have now turned their backs on the Holy Bible and turned their backs on the four Gospels—the most important four books in the whole world. Therefore, they have not found their salvation, nor a loving God that has made it possible to know and learn of His Son as the only way to be saved. But instead, they have closed their own door to Jesus—Who is the door to eternal life.

CHAPTER FIVE

Finding the Tomb of Jesus

"Great Stone at Mount Nebo[16]"— the missing link to the true tomb of Jesus has now been discovered!

> Mark 16:4 *And when they looked, they saw that the stone was rolled away:* ***for it was very great***.

Based on my research and findings, the *Holy Sepulchre* is NOT the true tomb of Jesus because the "Great Stone" proves it only fits one tomb in the whole world, *"The Garden Tomb."* In my research and discovery[17], I came across a Christian video showing what they call, "The Abu Badd - Rolling stone once used as a fortified door." I had to go see it for myself! After having visited the tomb— testing and measuring it against this "Rolling Stone,"—it matched! The GREAT Missing Stone was found, therefore locating the true tomb of Jesus. You can watch more in my video documentary[15].

The Rolling Stone

A Picture of "The Great Stone"

Acts 13:41 Look, you scoffers, wonder and perish, for I am going to do something in your days that you would never believe, even if someone told you.

Mark 16:4 And when they looked, they saw that the stone was rolled away: for it was very GREAT.

Some People Are Misled

So many people are misled and confused and do not know what the true tomb of Jesus is, just as so many are with regards to the Shroud.

Let's address this issue and understand the problem. The finger of blame is pointing in entirely the wrong direction. The question is: **"Is the Shroud Genuine?"**

Now let's address the problem properly, without condemning the good with the bad, but confirming to seekers that these things are genuine and true and to be used for the good.

As born again believers, we are to love all people God created—including our enemies and those of different religions—but hate what they stand for and doctrines that go against the truth, the gospel of Jesus Christ.

Biblical doctrine is important, as this doctrine equals truth.

> John 13:34 *A new commandment I give unto you, That ye love one another; as I have loved you, that ye also love one another.*

> Psalm 119:142 *Thy righteousness is an everlasting righteousness, and thy law is the truth.*

Some say, "I don't need to believe *The Shroud of Turin* is real." And I say, "That's great. But what about those who don't know the Lord? Wouldn't you think that some proof of His existence might help them make a soul-saving decision?" Sadly, for some like my wife and I, even our own parents believe Jesus is a fairy tale.

> Hosea 4:6 *My people are destroyed for lack of knowledge: because thou hast rejected knowledge, I will also reject thee, that thou shalt be no priest to me: seeing thou hast forgotten the law of thy God, I will also forget thy children.*

In fact, my wife and I posted around 100 leaflets in people's doors in our neighborhood offering FREE Christian films. We even spoke to some, but not one person was interested in learning about Jesus. Instead, we made new enemies we never had. Now they ignore us and turn the other way when we pass them on the street. So we pray and trust the Lord to bless them and hope that at some point they may become born again.

One only needs to think about Saul of Tarsus who abused the early Christian believers. He later became the great Apostle Paul and wrote half of the New Testament in the Holy Bible. But everything came about for him in God's perfect timing. There are many Saul types out there; however, we need to see their potential as the Lord sees them.

> 2 Peter 3:9 *The Lord is not slack concerning his promise, as some men count slackness; but is longsuffering to usward, not willing that any should perish, but that all should come to repentance.*

> Hebrews 1:14 *Are they not all ministering spirits (Angels), sent forth to minister for them **who shall be** heirs of salvation?*

Very clearly most of the world would do well to examine the physical evidence of the Shroud and examine the written evidence in the Bible that could lead them to accept the Lord Jesus as their Savior, too. That is why

I wrote this book to get the truth out there to help people make a soul-saving decision. It's my desire to help people surrender their souls to Jesus, and if one person seeing the evidence of our Risen Savior will help them, then this book has done what it was sent to do.

Good and Bad

Does God destroy good people with the bad? No.

We know from the well-known stories of Sodom and Gomorrah in Genesis 19:24 and Noah's Ark in Genesis 6:5 that God removed the good first and Joshua 6:25, where Rahab and her family were saved out of the destruction Jericho. But before He destroyed the bad He used the good to glorify His Word—just as God is going to do in these last days. He will again remove the good and destroy the bad.

> Matthew 13:30 *Let both grow together until the harvest: and in the time of harvest I will say to the reapers, Gather ye together first the tares, and bind them in bundles to burn them: but gather the wheat into my barn.*

> Matthew 3:12 *Whose fan is in his hand, and he will thoroughly purge his floor, and gather his wheat into the garner; but he will burn up the chaff with unquenchable fire.*

This is why we need not fear what the world is doing. God is our shield and buckler, and He delivers us from destruction. Though we may be on the Titanic, the Lord Jesus is our lifeboat, and we will be rescued.

Just as all believers should do with the Shroud" Use it for good to glorify God and His Word, which perhaps may help bring a lost soul to the saving grace of Jesus Christ.

Sadly

It is very clear that certain fundamentalist Christian ministries have led seekers down the wrong path by their sloppy research on *The Shroud of Turin* and have failed to understand and reveal the truth.

> Romans 8:28 *And we know that all things work together for good to them that love God, to them who are the called according to his purpose.*

I tuned into a live Christian television program one day, and the teacher was asked, "Is the Shroud genuine?" Eager to hear his response, I was shocked by his response. He said it couldn't be genuine because there was only one cloth discovered, not two. We see that this person, as a leading Christian teacher, clearly did not do his research.

Most don't understand that there were two cloths discovered, which have been proven by DNA to have both been used on the same body.

On certain Christian web sites it is said that the Shroud is a hoax, because the Bible states that Jesus was wrapped in strips of linen, concluding that the Shroud cannot be genuine because it is one cloth and not strips. They are getting confused with the ones that bound Lazarus, or they have seen too many mummy movies. We see here more sloppy conclusions by individuals who have not done their research well. They don't believe themselves so consequently mislead other people from believing the truth.

It is most shocking and sad for so many

who are seeking the truth to come across these individuals only to be led astray, and in turn, misinform others.

The problem here is that bad seeds bear bad fruit. Jesus clearly warns us about this...

> Matthew 7:16-20 *[16]Ye shall know them by their fruits. Do men gather grapes of thorns, or figs of thistles? [17]Even so every good tree bringeth forth good fruit; but a corrupt tree bringeth forth evil fruit. [18]A good tree cannot bring forth evil fruit, neither can a corrupt tree bring forth good fruit. [19]Every tree that bringeth not forth good fruit is hewn down, and cast into the fire. [20]Wherefore by their fruits ye shall know them.*

It is also vital to some who need further evidence to be informed correctly to strengthen their faith. Evidence of God and the Bible strengthens a believer's foundations.

The stronger one's faith is, the greater it will be to carry us through our trials. Every Bible discovery that reveals evidence of God's Holy Word is like a knock-out-punch on our greatest and most evil enemy—Satan—who is at work to deceive us from the truth and ultimately try and destroy us.

> John 10:10 *The thief cometh not, but for to steal, and to kill, and to destroy:*

Good evidence of Jesus, such as the Shroud, can bring many lost souls to Jesus Himself — the Solid Rock and foundation.

If we do our research properly, just as the Apostle Dr. St. Luke did by being a great researcher, afforded him opportunity to travel with St. Paul. He was privileged to meet people who knew Jesus personally like Mary, the mother of Jesus, St. John and Matthew. St. Luke's proper research has paid off well, for he was able to reveal unique teachings of Christianity only found in his writings, "The Gospel of St. Luke."

CHAPTER SIX

The Linen Cloths

Just by looking into the Greek translations, we come closer to understanding the truth. In my research, the word that is found in the Greek is translated in English to "linen cloths."

The word: "Cloths" in the Greek = ὀθόνια

English = linen cloths

What does it say about the burial cloths of Jesus?

> John 20:6 *Then came Simon Peter following him, and went into the sepulchre, and saw the linen **cloths** lying.*

We find there is not one mention of strips being used, but rather linen cloths—"plural"—supporting evidence that there is more than one, and that a cloth is a piece of material, not strips. To see this clearly, we need to define what a *cloth* is:

The on-line Dictionary[18] says: A fabric formed by weaving, felting, etc., from wool, hair, silk, flax, cotton, or other fiber, used for garments, upholstery, and many other items.

So it has to be a large piece of material, not strips as some may think. This has to be clear here, because this once again proves that there were "cloths" that were found in the tomb.

And what does St. Luke say speaking of Jesus' body?

> Luke 23:53 *And having taken it down, he wrapped it in a clean linen cloth.*

Please note, "A clean linen cloth."

Unfortunately, in some of the newer Bible translations we find the word "strips" instead of "cloths." (New International Version ©1984).

> John 20:6 (NIV) *Then Simon Peter, who was behind him, arrived and went into the tomb. He saw the **strips** of linen lying there.*

Certain believers have used the wrong translations that contain the wrong word "strips" instead of the right words "linen cloths" for their main argument to wrongly debunk *The Shroud of Turin*.

Personally, in the past I have not used the King James Bible exclusively and have often used the Greek Bible. However, I am aware now that there are several versions of Greek Translations that we must also consider. We have our work cut out for us if we want to get to the real truth.

Pastor Caspar McCloud[19] (Pastor of the Upper Room Fellowship in Canton, GA) has done extensive research of Bible translations and states: "All the modern translations based on the work of Westcott and Hort have done nothing but bring confusion into the church. Let us stay with the reliable Masoretic Text with the Septuagint influence, known as The Authorized Version, commonly better known as the King James Version. The Word of God has not changed, but it shall change us as we discover the Gospel truth."

Sudarium of Oviedo and The Shroud of Turin

Both cloths were proved to have covered the same body. Blood tests conducted on the *Sudarium of Oviedo* and *The Shroud of Turin* prove that both are of the same blood type—AB—a rare blood type amongst medieval Europeans and mostly common in the Middle East.

It is clear God has shown His love and determination to save the human race He created by proving and strengthening believers and unbelievers the same by preserving and revealing rock-solid evidence of His only begotten Son—outside the Bible—as a 3D negative hologram on a single piece of cloth!

The rock-solid evidence exists—evidence of an event that we, who are yet alive, and all those since the time when Jesus was crucified did not see with our own eyes. Yet, we can still see the proof 2000 years later of his time on earth—the scourging, crucifixion, death, and resurrection of Jesus the Christ (Yeshua), the promised Messiah. Evidence preserved so that future generations may study it and come to believe that could lead to their salvation.

Again, there are many, including believers, that have done their best to condemn the only physical, visible evidence that shows Jesus lived, was crucified, and resurrected. However we also have evidence from a number of secular writers of that time period who wrote about Jesus of Nazareth, such as Flavius Josephus[20] (born 34 AD).

Flavius was a Jewish historian who became a Pharisee at the age of 19 and later Commander of the Jewish forces in Galilee. He was captured by the Romans and ended up writing an historical account of his time period.

And I quote:

"Now there was about this time Jesus, a wise man if it be lawful to call him a man, for he was a doer of wonderful works, a teacher of such men as receive the truth with pleasure. He drew over to him both many Jews, and many of the Gentiles. He was the Christ, and when Pilate, at the suggestion of the principal men among us, had condemned Him to the cross, those that loved Him at the first, did not forsake Him; for he appeared to them alive again the third day; as the divine prophets had foretold these and ten thousand other wonderful things concerning Him. And the tribe of Christians so named from him are not extinct at this day."

In my many emails I have received, here is one from an atheist. He wrote saying, "Hey guys guess what, god isn't real. Show me one piece of evidence one piece, that god is real."

And here is another one from another individual saying, "What a crock of B.S., the Bible was written by humans and rewritten numerous times."

We can see by this person's request he is asking for one piece of evidence of God. But because there is doubt that the Shroud is real, he may struggle and not come to the knowledge of the truth, thereby condemning Him to hell.

In a book called, "Flight to Heaven[21]" there is a quote I read that says: "Knowledge is flawed, but truth prevails." This is very accurate according to the Bible.

> 2 Timothy 3:7 *Ever learning, and never able to come to the knowledge of the truth.*

Knowledge is plentiful today, but the knowledge that many are getting is not the truth. 1 Corinthians 8:1 says that knowledge puffs us up—in other words, filled with pride—instead of filling us with love.

> 1 Corinthians 8:1 *Now as touching things offered unto idols, we know that we all have knowledge. Knowledge puffeth up, but charity edifieth.*

It seems clear to me why God has given us the Shroud—to use it as rock-solid evidence to prove the Bible was inspired by God. By teaching the authenticity of the Shroud, we can show these guys the evidence they are looking for. And I say, "Now turn from your sins and believe."

It is puzzling how one can believe in Jesus Christ of Nazareth and yet teach people that the only piece of evidence that we have of Him and can be physically seen—outside the Bible—is a lying, deceiving fake.

The Shroud of Turin Speaks for Itself

It seems to be fundamentalist ministries who use scientific archeological evidence to prove the Bible, yet they teach that the most important and greatest archeological evidence is a hoax. As Barrie once stated, "People accept the one piece of evidence against the Shroud." But throw out the 99% of the evidence for the Shroud.

The Shroud played a part in the most important time in history. Are we that mad to believe that this cloth, that was closer to the body of Jesus than anything else for three whole days, would have been lost or forgotten?

When a family member dies, most of us keep some of their closest items. In my case, when my mother passed away, I took possession of her portable phone book.

The very fact that no human being could create the Shroud can only mean one thing, that God must have made this 3D cloth of Jesus Himself. This, then, raises an important question... If God made it, why would He then want us to teach and tell seekers it is a forgery? Does our GREAT God do things by mistake? No! It is clear that it is God's desire for the world to be reminded of His love for the world.

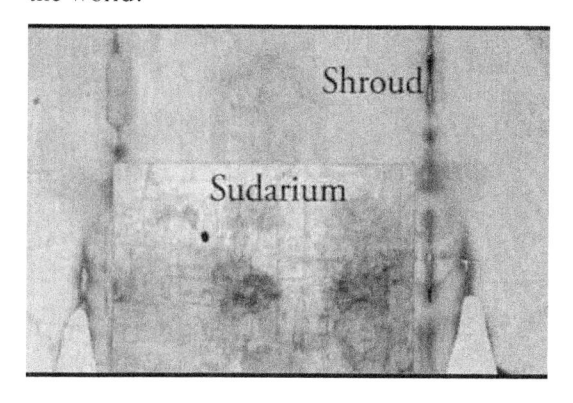

©1978 Barrie M. Schwortz Collection, STERA, Inc., All Rights Reserved

Chapter Seven

What is the Point of the Shroud?

As Dr. LA Marzull[22] once told me: "The Shroud is God's calling card."

Carole Bevan-Iryby[23] stated, "The Shroud is God's love letter on a cloth."

Dr. Richard Kent of *The Final Frontier*[24] once told me: "Ask the skeptics this question... Who can create a photo-negative 3D image on a single cloth even with today's technology?"

"Many have tried, with ridiculous results," said Barrie M. Schwortz.

Dr. Richard Kent continues to say: "The actually proves the resurrection of Jesus Christ. The image on the Shroud can be explained by the Bible, and an application of known laws of Theoretical Physics, and is a scorch in photo-negative, caused by radiation, with the appearance of an X-ray, but with additional distance imaging properties."

Chuck Missler[25] of Koinonia House Inc. states: "Dame Piczek, a Hungarian trained particle physicist and internationally renowned monumental artist, has apparently uncovered hard, scientific evidence of the Shroud. She contends that the image was created in an infinitesimally small fraction of a second and its formation was absent of the effects of gravity. Dame Piczek explains the complicated physics behind the image on the Shroud saying: *As quantum time collapses to absolute zero [time stopped moving] in the tomb of Christ, the two event horizons, one stopping events from above and the other stopping the events from below at the moment of the zero time collapse going through the body, get infinitely close to each other and eliminate each other, causing the image to print itself on the two sides of the Shroud."*

When expert photographer Barrie M. Schwortz first saw the Shroud, he was expecting to walk away laughing after seeing clear evidence of a painting. However, it shocked and proved him wrong—realizing that it was a 3D image, and not a painting on the cloth. After years of dedicated research, he discovered the Shroud could not have possibly been created by the hands of a man, which would then change his whole life and come to establish him as the greatest expert on the burial cloth of Jesus.

Barrie said his Mum once told him, "Of course the Shroud is authentic! If it belonged to any one else, no one would have cared or would have kept it."

And Barrie's son once told him, "You can see the Shroud is not a painting, because you can only see the image of Jesus at a distance, but not close up to it. How can one paint a painting if one cannot see what they are painting?" Out of the mouths of babes...

Barrie also stated that his Jewish friends had more faith that it was Jesus on the cloth than many Christians.

In a recent interview with Barrie, he made the statement to Emma and myself, "When you look at the Shroud, how could we not love Jesus?" I say Amen and Amen.

Pastor Caspar McCloud says: "The Lord used the Shroud to help convert me in the late 1970's and I dare say probably many more people over the years who realized that Jesus was real. Why are there so many intelligent scholarly types who also believe this is, in fact, the genuine article the Bible speaks of? Are we to say that suddenly now God is not able to do the impossible and leave us the imprint of the Glorious Resurrection of our Lord Jesus?

Luke 1:37 *For with God nothing shall be impossible.*

Let us learn to simplify our message to an unsaved world. The message in the Holy Bible is not complicated: **Come to Christ**. In fact, we the body of Christ as the priesthood of believers, are the body of Christ. So let us take the Gospel message everywhere we go with signs and wonders—cloths and aprons, for example—just as His followers did in the book of Acts,

Yes, wonders, healings and miracles will follow us as we follow after the Lord Jesus (Yeshua). To God be all the glory. Many religious people will not be allowed into Heaven, as described in Revelation 17. After all, the Lord Jesus rebuked five out of the seven churches named in Revelation chapters two and three.

Dr. Peter Soons[26], a 3D imaging expert, states: "The Shroud of Turin is one huge message—a gift of God to the world. The science of the Shroud proves that Jesus Christ existed, was crucified and resurrected exactly as written down 2000 years ago."

Frederick T. Zugibe[27] (M.S., M.D., Ph.D., FCAP, FACC, FAAFS) studied the Shroud and crucifixion for over 50 years and was responsible for many ground-breaking results in his research. Among them he was:

1. First to determine that the cause of death in crucifixion was due to hypovolemic and traumatic shock and not due to asphyxiation.

2. First to show that the straightening and sagging theory on the cross is physically impossible.

3. First to show that the so called bifurcation image pattern was not due to a change in angle of the wrists and not due to straightening and sagging.

4. First to show that the nails pierced the upper part of the palms of the hands and not through the wrists.

5. First to measure the exact pull on the hands during crucifixion when the feet are secured, utilizing highly sophisticated, state of the art, strain-tension equipment and to show that the tension formula (two times the cosine of the angle of the arms with the upright of the cross) that had been universally accepted is not applicable to crucifixion when the feet are secured to the upright of the cross.

6. First to refute and prove incorrect, the widely held hypothesis that injury to the median nerve was the reason that the thumbs do not show on the Shroud and also to demonstrate why this was so.

Mechthild Flury-Lemberg discovery[28]

Mechthild Flury-Lemberg, as I mentioned earlier, is a Swiss textile restorer and expert who studied weaving at an academy in Hamburg, Germany and earned degrees in the History of Art from universities in Kiel and Munich. She agreed in 2002 to head the restoration and conservation of the linen Shroud and discovered clear evidence that the Shroud was the work of a professional and is surprisingly similar to the hem of a cloth found in the tombs of the Jewish fortress of Masada. The Masada cloth dates between 40 B.C. and 73 A.D.

She also discovered that *The Shroud of Turin* was of an extraordinary quality and could only be purchased by a rich man like Joseph of Arimathea—precisely what we are told happened in the Gospels.

Look at the 120 scourge marks on the body, front and back—consistent with "40 lashes"—and the crucified holes in His feet and wrists. What do you see? We see how much God loved us.

This is the back of *The Shroud of Turin* where I added the bloodstains consistent with the 40 lashes, and around 120 scourge marks on the front and back of the body by a three-thonged whip. Experts who have studied the Shroud agree. (See more on my film called, "The Evidence and The True Face of The Shroud.")

What is the Point of the Shroud?

©1978 Barrie M. Schwortz Collection, STERA, Inc.,
All Rights Reserved

I am quite sure of my calling and work on the Shroud and therefore feel committed to see it through, believing it is the greatest and most powerful tool that proves and confirms God's Son, Jesus Christ, and His Holy Word written down in the scriptures. I do not believe there is a greater tool for demolishing, smashing, and tearing down the barriers erected against the truth of Jesus Christ.

If only the unbelieving believers would use the Shroud to prove the reliability of the Bible and the physical evidence of the life of Jesus—His agony and bloodshed, His pierced hands and feet, His cross and passion, His crucifixion, death, and burial, and His resurrection—instead of trying to prove to the world

The Shroud of Turin Speaks for Itself

that the earth is only 6000 years old.

It seems like the unbelieving believers who condemn the Shroud got on the wrong boat and are missing the point. Believers would bring far more lost souls to Jesus by showing the world the physical evidence of Jesus, rather than arguing with the world that it was created in seven days 6000 years ago. By believing this, it does not save souls, but believing and following Jesus down the right path does.

It is wrong for ministries to interfere with other ministries' rightful work when defending the truth of our Lord Jesus. However, it doesn't matter how much I have been attacked and hated for believing in the Shroud, I will remember the last words of Jesus on the cross when He said: *"Father forgive them, for they know not what they do."*

If you are one of these, I forgive you and love you.

Please, let us pray that the eyes open for those *doubting Thomas's* who are grieving God's heart. The cloths were left behind to show us His love for the world, and we will make good from it, instead, by shouting from the roof tops that *The Shroud of Turin* proves by the scourging marks of crucifixion impregnated on the cloths, the resurrected Jesus Christ (Yeshua), the promised Messiah.

It proves the Holy Bible to be forensically accurate and perfectly reliable in every possible way and in every detail truthful concerning the most important event in human history—the crucifixion of Jesus, the greatest miracle in the world, the Resurrection of Yeshua.

> If you are looking for the evidence of Jesus, here it is. It is time to turn away from our sins, believe and receive salvation, and follow Jesus. Amen.

Chapter Eight

Pastor Caspar McCloud
co-author

Message of the Resurrection of Jesus Christ of Nazareth

Pastor Caspar McCloud's research will help bring understanding about Jesus' life and the power of His resurrection. I felt it important because, without the resurrection, everything we do is in vain.

> 1 Corinthians 15:6 *After that, he was seen of above five hundred brethren at once; of whom the greater part remain unto this present, but some are fallen asleep.*

After the most significant and amazing resurrection of all history—when Jesus Christ of Nazareth, Messiah (Yeshua), came back to life—He brought many of the Old Testament Saints back with Him.

> Matthew 27:52-53 *[52]And the graves were opened; and many bodies of the saints which slept arose, [53]And came*

out of the graves after his resurrection, and went into the holy city, and appeared unto many.

These resurrected saints must have had real bodies. There are actually several ancient documents that confirm this. For example: Simon, the temple priest who had waited to see the baby Jesus before he died, had two sons who lived in Arimathea. The records state that the Sanhedrin specifically investigated any resurrections, as they were common in that day.

It is stated in the records from the Ante-Nicene Library that both sons of Simon were interrogated separately and at the same time, and both had given the same kind of explanation. They both claimed that Jesus Christ of Nazareth, Messiah (Yeshua), had appeared to them in Hades where He preached a message to everyone who had died and was there. I can make an educated guess what He preached, as Jesus took that repentant thief with Him and shared about the New Covenant. He also probably taught from the Holy Scriptures how those Old Testament saints would accompany Him back to Heaven and all those who refused to obey the Voice of God and the Lord's prophets must remain there until the judgment.

The records from the accounts stored in the Ante-Nicene Library state that the Lord Jesus then took these two brothers—along with all those Old Testament Saints who believed the Lord—and were given new, resurrected bodies as Christ, Who resurrected out of that Tomb. The Bible clearly tells us that many came out of the graves and went into Jerusalem at this time. It also says Jesus appeared to many of His followers, as we just saw in Matthew 27:52-53.

According to the writings of Jewish historian, Flavius Josephus, and Roman records during this Passover, one sheep would serve as a sacrifice for only 5 people. There were at least another 100,000 people who had entered the city of already 250,000 people who lived there. You can just imagine how much sacrificial lamb's blood was spilled that day.

But it's only by the blood of God's Lamb, Jesus, that we have Salvation. God chose to connect Jesus (Yeshua), with Passover in His perfect timing that we might understand. Is it any wonder that John the Baptist introduces

Jesus by saying, "Behold, the Lamb!" It's no wonder Paul writes "Christ, our Passover Lamb, has been slain!" Because Passover is all about Jesus (Yeshua)!

- Jesus came as the LAMB of God!
- His Blood redeems US!
- By His Blood… He covers our confessed sins.
- By His Blood…the power of the enemy is broken!
- By His Blood…we are released from bondage and oppression and all sickness and diseases.
- By His Blood…we are made free to enter into Papa God's Promise!

Pastor Caspar closes his message by saying, "Passover is about the Celebration of our Lord Jesus, and *The Shroud of Turin* is a wonderful piece of physical evidence of His suffering and mission."

Conclusion

The whole purpose of this study and discovery is to help bring people to the saving grace of Jesus Christ. Some need evidence; others do not. I hope that the evidence shown in this book helps you make a decision for the Lord.

When we "believe" that Jesus Christ truly died on the cross for our sins, and if we believe that Jesus rose from the dead and follow Him by taking up our cross, we shall be saved.

1 Thessalonians 4:14 *For if we believe that Jesus died and rose again, even so them also which sleep in Jesus will God bring with him.*

Luke 9:23 *And he said to them all, If any man will come after me, let him deny himself, and take up his cross daily, and follow me.*

Some need physical proof...well, here it is. The Bible says, "Blessed are those who have not seen, yet hath believed." Whether or not you believe what I shared in this book, if you have not yet received this free gift of salvation through Jesus Christ our Lord, now is the day!

Prayer For Salvation

God promises if you put your trust in Him and believe in His Son, Jesus Christ, the time will come when He will wipe away every tear from your eyes. And there will be no more pain or suffering ever again. God will pour out His love for you forever. Do you want to be a part of God's family? Then surrender your heart to God.

Say this prayer with me, and this prayer will change your life. This prayer will change your destination to come. And this prayer will be the most important event in your life—the most important words you have ever said. Repeat the following out loud (The reason we pray out loud is Romans 10:9 says to make your confession with your mouth):

"Dear God, the Father, I know that I have broken Your laws and my sins have hurt you. I am truly sorry, and now I want to turn away from my past sinful life toward You. Please forgive me, and help me avoid sinning again. I believe that Your Son,

Jesus Christ, died for my sins, was resurrected from the dead, is alive, and hears my prayer. I invite Jesus to become the Lord of my life, to rule and reign in my heart from this day forward. Please send me Your Holy Spirit to help me obey You and to do Your will for the rest of my life. In Jesus' Name I pray, Amen."

Now seek God with all your heart, otherwise just saying this prayer will not accomplish anything on its own.

My Prayer for You

"Lord, because of your people's prayers right now, and as one of Your representatives, I take the authority You have given me, and I break every curse that has been hindering this person who had sincerely prayed this. I revoke any curses now, and I release them from each one in the Name of Jesus Christ of Nazareth. In His all prevailing Name I declare these people released.

Satan, I declare to you this day that you have no more claims, no more access to their lives, to their families, and their business. They have been lifted out of the domain of darkness and translated into the Kingdom of the Son of God's almighty love.

Father in Heaven, I ask You to fill them with Your perfect peace, Your love and Your compassion, so they can in turn love You, love themselves, and love others. Help them to forgive every person in their life that has ever hurt them or offended them. By putting their trust in You, they will be freed from all sin and given the power to live this life with joy. In Jesus' Name I pray, Amen."

Now go and tell what God has done for you! Your testimony needs to be shared, and we would love to hear it ourselves. Revelation 12:11 says that the Blood of the Lamb and the word of our testimony can defeat the enemy.

For further studies on salvation go to:
http://www.realdiscoveries.info/
SurrendertoGod.php

If you received Jesus Christ as your personal Savior today, start your new life by picking up the Instructional Guide Book to the supernatural—the Holy Bible—as your personal God-inspired Bill of Rights, and give it first place in your life.

Supernatural peace in your life will increase as you increase in the knowledge of God's Will and His Word. (Proverbs 4:4-13, 20-22).

> *Jesus said unto him, I am the way, the truth, and the life: no man comes unto the Father, but by me.*
>
> John 14:6

About the Author
Simon Brown

Simon Brown, a born again believer and the author of the Real Discoveries web sites. org., com. and info. has produced four feature documentaries which are aired on Sky TV. He is mostly known for his first film, "Our Search for Sodom and Gomorrah"—which is probably the most watched film on *YouTube* in its category.

He believes God has also led him to some important archeological discoveries. His main discovery was in 2011 when he believed God revealed to him the Great Stone as told in Mark 16:4 which proved to be the missing link to the true tomb of Jesus.

Simon produced his second film, "Our Search for the Tomb of Jesus," revealing a great deal of evidence in support of the Garden Tomb. His find on the Great Stone at Mount Nebo proved his previous research on the tomb of Jesus to be accurate and reliable.

His third film is called, "Our Search for Real Discoveries Around the Dead Sea." Simon then produced his fourth film," The Evidence and The True Face of The Shroud," which aired on Sky TV.

Simon and his wife, Emma, have a passion to prove that the Bible is true, reliable, and accurate.

Simon has a desire to share what knowledge and understanding he has been granted. Through his websites and the information offered, he hopes to open the eyes of those who do not fully realize the importance of the Bible and its teachings.

Emma, his wife, plays a large part in all this by working with Simon.

Recently, many discoveries have been made—especially in the Holy Land—which support the Bible's account of history.

That is precisely what "Real Discoveries" is all about.

Photos of Emma and Simon with sulphur balls found at Sodom and Gomorrah.

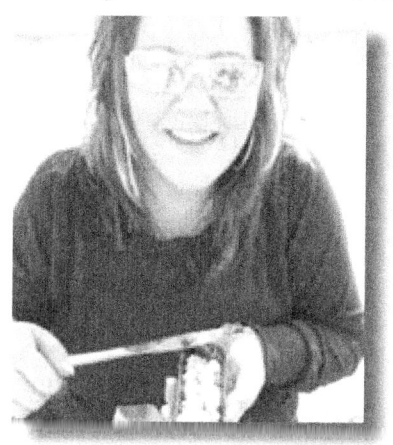

About the Co-Author
Caspar McCloud

Caspar McCloud is an outstanding virtuoso guitarist, singer and songwriter, an accomplished portrait artist, as well as equestrian, ordained minister and author of three books, *"The revised* "Nothing Is Impossible," which is his autobiography of healing and miracles, and, " What Was I Thinking?" published by Destiny Image, with co author Linda Lange, about how your thought life effects your mental, physical, relational and emotional health. "Exposing the Spirit of Self-Pity" that helps people to break free from past hurts and offences to find the more abundant life the Lord wants for them (John 10:10).

McCloud signed to Atlantic Records after leaving his home in England for New York City. He presently pastors a fellowship called, "The Upper Room Fellowship," in Canton GA, when he is not out traveling as a musician and guest speaker.

He is a husband and father of two, and spends his time studying to show himself approved of the Lord, riding his horse, taking care of his home and his flock, and ministering internationally. He has a heart to see people free, even you!

As a contributing staff writer for Dr. LA Marzulli's magazine PP&S ("Politics, Prophecy and the Supernatural). Dr. Marzulli suggested to Caspar to see the wonderful research Simon and Emma Brown were doing on *The Shroud of Turin* just after McCloud returned from ministering in UK in 2012. Through a series of events the Lord orchestrated and arranged for McCloud and the Browns to connect. Since then they have become close friends. In Simon's own words, "After praying for healing and guidance by God, we have been connected with a brother in Christ that we did not realize we had," Simon then posted an article on his website, http://www.realdiscoveries.org about the freedom and insights he was receiving since their friendship began.

McCloud also sent his friend Roy Wiley in Dover, to bring the Browns some of his books and music CD's believing they would also be helpful to minister to the Browns, and their friends. Appreciating McCloud's pastoral and scientific insights along with his gift of written communication, Simon asked his mate Caspar to help expand and enhance an article he was writing on *The Shroud of Turin*, which has now been adopted into this book. May it help bring you ever closer to the Lord Jesus Christ of Nazareth/Messiah Yeshua.

FREE DVD Offer!

The Evidence and the True Face of the Shroud film

Script By Matthew Tulloch Produced By Simon Brown

Barrie Schwortz, who is perhaps the world's greatest expert on the Shroud of Turin, is interviewed.

Barrie M. Schwortz STERA, Inc.

He gives lectures around the world and has appeared on the History Channel and National Geographic channel as a shroud expert, as well as in *Time Magazine*, *Newsweek*, *Life Magazine* and *National Geographic*, and many national and international news programs. Barrie also maintains the most authoritative site on the internet about the Shroud of Turin—www.shroud.com—which has been going for over fifteen years now.

Barrie states, "I just watched the program,

and it is excellent!"

This program discusses in accurate detail the scientific facts about the Shroud of Turin that show it is truly authentic. It addresses the infamous 1988 radiocarbon dating of the cloth that declared it medieval in origin and disputes those results with new scientific information that has come to light in recent years. It provides the viewer with an honest appraisal of what is truly known about the Shroud and does so in an interesting and honest manner.

To receive your free DVD go to:
www.realdiscoveries.info/
FREEDVDFILMS.php

All you pay for is the shipping costs!

Other Books and Resources

"Our Search for the Tomb of Jesus"

This book is our search for the real tomb of Jesus. You will learn about the real crucifixion site and more!

To read this book for free, go to: http://www.realdiscoveries.org/modules/articles/item.php?itemid=242

"Our Search for Sodom and Gomorrah"

Retired businessman Simon Brown went searching for the biblical cities of Sodom & Gomorrah. Read about these amazing discoveries and the compelling evidence that he found.

To read this book for free go to: http://www.realdiscoveries.org/modules/articles/item.php?itemid=178

"Our Search for Real Discoveries"

In this book, Simon's team return to Sodom and Gomorrah for a closer look. They also searched for Admah and Zoar, the surrounding towns.

To read this book for free, go to http://www.realdiscoveries.org/modules/articles/item.php?itemid=245

For more exciting discoveries, visit us at:

http://www.realdiscoveries.info
RealDiscoveries.com
RealDiscoveries.org
RealDiscoveries.tv
RealDiscoveries2.com
ParablesOfJesusEpisodes.com
TheGardenTombAndTheGreatStone.com
Real Discoveries You Tube Channel

Contact Information

Please contact us at:

Real Discoveries
Simon Brown
www.realdiscoveries.info
email:mrsimonbrown@aol.com

Pastor Caspar McCloud Ministries Inc.
1901 Batesville Rd.
Canton, GA 30115
http://www.theupperroomfellowship.org
email: pastorcaspar@gmail.com

Footnotes References

1. Joe Marino - http://shroudstory.com/2011/01/19/joe-marino-sue-benford-and-the-carbon-dating-of-the-shroud-of-turin/
2. Ray Rogers - http://cybercomputing.com/freeinquiry//skeptic/shroud/articles/rogers-ta-response.htm
3. Pete Shumaker - http://www.einterface.net/gamini/shroudinfo.html
4. Barrie Schwortz - http://www.youtube.com/watch?v=YHaMEOPvbUA
5. Barrie Schwortz - http://www.shroud.com
6. Cordex Pray - www.codexsinaiticus.org; http://greatshroudofturinfaq.com/History/Greek-Byzantine/Pray-Codex/
7. Montreal Gazette - http://newbuddhist.com/discussion/13506/the-turin-shroud-could-not-have-been-faked-say-scientists)
8. TBN documentary - http://www.tbn.org/watch-us/our-programs/our-search-for-the-tomb-of-jesus) called, "Our search for the tomb of Jesus"
9. Simon Brown's website: www.realdiscoveries.com

10. Mechthild Flury-Lemberg - http://www.newgeology.us/presentation24.html
11. http://en.wikipedia.org/wiki/Sudarium_of_Oviedo
12. Ark holding the Sudarium - http://en.wikipedia.org/wiki/File:Arca_santa_de_Oviedo.JPG
13. http://en.wikipedia.org/wiki/Shroud_of_Turin
14. Ben Stein - http://topdocumentaryfilms.com/expelled-no-intelligence-allowed/
15. C. Bernard Ruffin - http://topdocumentaryfilms.com/expelled-no-intelligence-allowed/
16. Mount Nebo - http://www.sacred-destinations.com/jordan/mount-nebo.htm
17. http://youtu.be/X8BqARq0pXw
18. Definition of cloth - (http://dictionary.reference.com/browse/cloth?s=t)
19. Pastor Caspar McCloud: www.casparmccloud.net
20. Flavius Josephus - http://christianbookshelf.org/josephus/the_antiquities_of_the_jews/chapter_3_sedition_of_the.htm
21. Flight to Heaven - http://www.amazon.com/Flight-Heaven-Crash-A-Survivor-A-Heaven/dp/0764207946

22. Dr. LA Marzull - http://lamarzulli.net/
23. Carole Bevan-http://www.carolebevanirby.com/home.php
24. http://www.finalfrontier.org.uk
25. http://www.khouse.org/articles/2009/847
26. http://shroud3d.com/findings/prof-avino-am-danin
27. Frederick T. Zugibe - http://www.e-forensicmedicine.net
28. http://www.pbs.org/wnet/secrets/previous_seasons/case_shroudchrist/interview.html
    http://www.shroud.com/pdfs/n65part4.pdf

Printed in Great Britain
by Amazon